SIGNS OF THE SEASONS

Signs of
Autumn

Paul Humphrey

Photography by Chris Fairclough

W
FRANKLIN WATTS
LONDON•SYDNEY

This edition 2006
© 2001 Franklin Watts

First published in Great Britain by
Franklin Watts
338 Euston Road
London NW1 3BH

Franklin Watts Australia
Level 17/207 Kent Street
Sydney NSW 2000

ISBN: 978 0 7496 6957 7

Dewey Decimal Classification 574.5
A CIP catalogue record for this book is available from the British Library

Printed in China

Planning and production by Discovery Books
Editors: Tamsin Osler, Samantha Armstrong
Design: Ian Winton
Art Director: Jonathan Hair

Photographs:
Bruce Coleman: 19 (Jane Burton);
Oxford Scientific Films: 6: (Ronald Toms), 22 (Bridget Wheeler), 23 Chris Knights).
All other photography by Chris Fairclough.

'Misty' from Out and About © 1988 Shirely Hughes
Reproduced by permission of the publisher, Walker Books Ltd, London.

Franklin Watts is a divison of Hachette Children's Books,
an Hachette Livre UK company.

CONTENTS

Autumn is coming. Look for the signs of autumn.

The weather is getting cooler. Sometimes
you have to put warm clothes on.

It can be misty in the mornings.

There is dew on the spider's web.

It can be windy
and rainy, too.

10

The rain fills the puddles.

You start a new school year in the autumn.

At school
you might
play football...

...or netball.

Leaves on the trees are changing colour...

...and falling to the ground.

The fallen leaves are food for worms.

Mushrooms and toadstools grow
in the damp grass.

Some trees are
covered in seeds.

They fall to
the ground.

18

There are acorns and nuts
on the ground, too.

The squirrels collect them.

You can collect conkers...

...and play with them.

The swallows gather on telephone wires...

...before they fly away to warmer places for the winter.

Wild geese arrive, leaving the snow and ice of colder lands.

Gardeners clean up their gardens...

...and make compost heaps and bonfires.

Farmers harvest their crops...

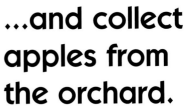

...and collect apples from the orchard.

What other signs of autumn can you see?

Misty

Mist in the morning,
Raw and nippy,
Leaves on the pavement,
Wet and slippy.

Sun on fire
Behind the trees,
Muddy boots,
Muddy knees.

Shop windows,
Lighted early,
Soaking grass,
Dewy, pearly.

Red, lemon,
Orange and brown,
Silently, softly,
The leaves float down.

Shirley Hughes

INDEX